learning
and
development
in
practice

HOW TO CREATE TRAINING PROGRAMS
THAT MAKE AN IMPACT

BY

NAZANIN TADJBAKHSH, PH.D.

Learning and Development in Practice
How to Create Training Programs That Make an Impact

This edition published 2020
Copyright © Nazanin Tadjbakhsh 2020

ISBN: 978-0-578-64380-9

Publisher: Jellyfresh Press

Testimonials

"Naz's writing captivated me from the first few sentences. She portrays learning and development in a way that is accessible to all, learners and practitioners alike. An absolute MUST READ for anyone who wants to deliver value to themselves, their clients, and their organizations!"

— Nairee Bedikian,
Learning & Development, The Walt Disney Company

"A very detailed, practical and useful material that I'll be able to apply at any time during my career as a practitioner. I'm thankful to finally find a book offering a high level program that I can easily adjust and implement successfully. With a learner-centric approach, empathizing with learners and other innovative techniques, Naz provides the missing link to creating effective training programs."

— Gonzalo Munoz,
Organizational Development Consultant

"Naz does an amazing job of giving the learner's experience a human touch. In this book, you learn how to put people first when creating training that will impact their lives in a profound way. I highly recommend this book to anyone who is looking to maximize the learner experience to drive business results."

— Hagi Fuentes, M.A.,
Organizational Development Consultant,
Think Differently LLC

"Being new to Learning and Organization Development, this book brings much insight and value to employee training. It brings a new meaning to composing training programs and allows for reflection from the learner's perspective. As a former student of Dr. Tadjbakhsh, I guarantee that her passion, knowledge, and learner-centric approaches will guide practitioners in delivering world-class, impactful training programs!"

— Kristopher Sandoval,
Talent Acquisition Specialist and
former student of Dr. Tadjbakhsh

Dedication

To my siblings.

Table of Contents

Introduction

One of my most treasured hobbies is attending plays, musicals and live performances. I am fascinated by how these art forms transcend everyday life and language to tell stories that deeply connect people more closely not just with one another, but also with ourselves. Attending live performances refresh and energize me, so I made a commitment in 2016 to treat myself at least three times a year to such things. I am grateful to have had opportunities to watch a variety of shows, from hits like *Rent* and *Aladdin* to local productions of masterpieces such as *Cambodian Rock Band*, *Once*, and *Little Black Shadows*. While each and every performance moves me in one way or another, I can say without even the shadow of a doubt that attending the American debut (2017) of Alma Deutscher at Symphony Silicon Valley was a performance that transformed me and changed my life's course.

I was captivated by the 13-year-old prodigy who's been oftentimes referred to as "the next Mozart." She wore a stunning fuchsia gown, relishing in the delight of playing her violin. Her eyes were closed with deep concentration. She'd furrow her eyebrows during dramatic points in the music, fully immersed in an enchanting composition. What remains as my most visceral memory from this performance, however, was Alma's dazzling smile. I could feel the genuine delight and joy she experienced while playing her violin. She was not afraid of making any mistakes or what the audience thought of her - she shined so bright just by being her authentic self, showcasing her natural talents unapologetically. No one could argue against the fact that she was an immensely gifted force of nature. What struck me in particular was that the source of this remarkable force was her unwavering self-assurance and generosity in sharing her gift with others. As a byproduct, people were left in awe...speechless, just like me. Alma inspired me to step out of my own shadow that I had cast upon myself. For so long, I had been dimming my own light because I did not want to intimidate others, but Alma made me realize that by doing this, I was actually doing a disservice to both myself and to others with whom I could share my gifts and talents.

My epiphany

I took some time to reflect on the times when I felt that I truly shined bright, unapologetically showcased my gifts, and found delight in the process. It occurred to me that this has always been when I've been asked to partner with others to design unforgettable learning experiences. I am grateful that this has been validated by others as well, because when it comes to learning and development, I am the first person clients, peers, business leaders and friends call when they want to create high-impact training programs in record time. Creating training programs has become my signature way of sharing my natural talents.

For the past several years now, many people have been confessing to me that they wish they could get into my head whenever I am working on training programs so that they can learn from me. I realized that writing this book could be my "Alma moment," an opportunity to share my gifts with others. More importantly, this book is the most scalable way to optimize my impact as a practitioner and teacher: by documenting and sharing my process and best practices with fellow learning practitioners so that they too can maximize *their* impact.

This book is for both learning and development newcomers and seasoned practitioners looking to elevate their learning game and optimize their impact when designing and deploying training programs. I wrote this book to help fellow learning practitioners perfect the craft of delivering world-class training programs so that we can maximize our impact in organizations.

What problem am I solving?

Throughout my career, I've seen clients come to me with the same fundamental problem time and time again: "I need to create a high-impact training session that delivers results...and oh, it can be no longer than 60 minutes because we can't have employees away from work for too long." Create meaningful change in 60 minutes? I will always be up for that challenge.

Granted, I've developed training sessions that are as short as seven minutes all the way to year-long cohort-style programs. Of the 50+ training programs I've designed, however, the vast majority of sessions have been approximately 60-90 minutes in length. To my knowledge, I am not aware of a standard rule for corporate training sessions to be 60-90 minutes. My personal philosophy is not to focus so much on time, but rather, to do whatever it takes in the amount of time needed to achieve the desired outcomes. Nonetheless, a session length of 60-90 minutes is what most of my clients usually request because they want to get a lot accomplished in minimal time with their investment.

I have worked with many leaders saying that the training absolutely cannot be longer than 60 minutes. While this is possible, there are often times when 60 minutes is not long enough for the topic if you want to make a meaningful impact. For example, I once worked with a client who needed to prepare leaders for a large change in the organization. My client was adamant that the session be no longer than one hour. However, when presenting my training blueprint to the client (more on that in Chapter 7), I was able to justify that with discussions and role-play activities, the client would be able to maximize the impact of the training by extending the session to 90 minutes. My client agreed that extending the session by 30 minutes would be a worthwhile investment. Clients are usually open to extending a training session if you have adequately prepared and created the appropriate business case to do so.

Let me be clear that extending training time is never about making sessions longer for no apparent reason, but rather, because doing so maximizes the impact that can be made in a given training session. I hope that this book helps fellow practitioners blow their clients and learners away by how much of an impact they can make in such little time. My vision is for this book to help practitioners deliver world-class training programs so that clients see the benefits of their investments in learning. In turn, I hope that this results in clients making continuous investments in learning because we help solve learner problems in ways that deliver business results.

My process enables practitioners to get things done quickly, but not at the sacrifice of quality. In fact, I always prioritize quality over speed. Luckily, I have managed to find a way for us practitioners to do both... simultaneously...really well.

According to Raymond A. Noe (2017), *training* "refers to a planned effort by a company to facilitate learning of job-related competencies, knowledge, skills, and behaviors by employees," and *learning* "refers to employees acquiring knowledge, skills, competencies, attitudes, or behaviors." While the difference could be easy to miss between these two definitions, there is a clear distinction between training and learning. Training is the mechanism by which a company facilitates learning for its employees. Learning is the employee-focused outcome whereby the learner, or employee, retains and applies what was covered in the training. This book approaches training and learning with a learner-centric approach, focusing on high-impact strategies that drive business results.

The greatest gift of all

My sixth grade teacher, Dr. Lauren D. Cohen, once said something that I will never forget and continue to hold close to this very day as a talent development practitioner: "The one thing no one can ever take away from you is what you've learned."

What an honor and gift it is for us learning practitioners to give something to people that can never be taken away.

RECOMMENDED READINGS

I have intentionally kept the scope of this book very specific, focusing on my personal best practices on how to create training programs that make an impact. Therefore, I want to recommend a reading list of excellent companion books that you can peruse in conjunction with my book if you are new to learning and development or want to shore up your skills as a practitioner:

1. Bens, I. (2012). *Facilitating with Ease! Core Skills for Facilitators, Team Leaders and Members, Managers, Consultants, and Trainers.* (3rd Edition).

2. Berger, W. (2014). *A More Beautiful Question: The Power of Inquiry to Spark Breakthrough Ideas.*

3. Block, P. (2011). *Flawless Consulting. A Guide to Getting Your Expertise Used.* (3rd Ed.).

4. Heath, C., & Heath, D. (2017). *The Power of Moments: Why Certain Experiences Have Extraordinary Impact.*

5. McCall, M. W. (1998). *High Flyers: Developing the Next Generation of Leaders.*

6. McCauley, C. D., DeRue, D.S., Yost, P.R., & Taylor S. (2013). *Experience-Driven Leader Development: Models, Tools, Best Practices, and Advice for On-the-Job Development.*

7. Noe, R. A. (2017). *Employee Training & Development* (7th Ed.).

8. Wick, C. Pollock, R. & Jefferson, A. (2015). The Six Disciplines of Breakthrough Learning: How to Turn Training and Development into Business Results. (3rd edition).

Chapter 1

Adopting a
Learner-Centric Approach

B ased on my experiences listening to and empathizing with learners, I've realized that unfortunately, the bar is set very low when it comes to learning experiences from the perspective of learners. I won't lie to you - this made me upset and disheartened. While it was disappointing at first that the bar has been set very low for training, I realized shortly after that this was a huge opportunity to change the game in learning and development. I believe that there is an immense opportunity for us as learning and development practitioners to reframe, change our mindsets, and consider rebranding ourselves as learning experience curators. In order to do this, we must first adopt a learner-centric approach.

What is a learner-centric approach?

I want to draw from a company you'll likely recognize to help frame the conversation about adopting a learner-centric approach: Nordstrom. Nordstrom has built a legendary brand and reputation for world class customer service and experience, prioritizing that all employees maintain and foster a customer-centric culture.

Nordstrom has been praised for empowering employees to truly adopt a customer-centric approach and mindset with its Inverted Pyramid hierarchy. The underpinning philosophy of the Inverted Pyramid posits that the most important decisions lie in the hands of those who are interfacing most closely with customers. This, in turn, ensures an outstanding in-store experience at Nordstrom.

Nordstrom's Inverted Pyramid puts customers at the top of the "hierarchy's" upside-down pyramid, shortly followed by front-line employees such as salespeople and customer service. While most company hierarchies naturally place the CEO at the top followed by Senior Vice Presidents/Vice Presidents, and so on, Nordstrom has quite literally flipped this concept upside-down with the CEO at the bottom of the hierarchy and front-line employees towards the top, hence the name "Inverted Pyramid." This image serves as a constant reminder that Nordstrom cannot exist without customers, and that those who are closest to serving customers, front-line employees, are of the utmost importance.

This customer-centric approach is reflected in workplace practices at the store, department, and team levels to ensure that front-line employees are equipped and empowered with whatever they need to excel for their customers. As a former Nordstrom employee, I can certainly validate that the company took this very seriously. Whenever I had questions for my leaders about any customer issues I was facing in the moment, I was oftentimes coached through each scenario with the magic question: "What options can you provide to your customer that will make them leave happier than when they came in?"

What a powerful question. My leaders empowered me to come up with creative options that were focused on creating outcomes where the customer would leave happier than when they came in. We would co-create potential solutions and solve the problem in real-time. It was not a prescriptive, one-size-fits-all approach. Rather, I was encouraged to use my best judgment for each customer's unique situation. This is only one of many examples demonstrating Nordstrom's ability to provide world-class customer service and fostering a service-oriented culture. Having customers and front-line employees at the top of their Inverted

Pyramid is not just something they talk about, but a way of being that is displayed in their day-to-day interactions and behaviors.

Similarly, we as learning practitioners must put our learners at the top of our own metaphorical inverted pyramid so that we embody a learner-centric approach. In order to truly adopt a learner-centered mindset, we as learning practitioners must keep the learner top of mind at all times. We must empathize with the learners we are brought on to serve. It is our duty to push ourselves to see things from their perspective so that we can serve them in the best ways possible. In order to help you get into this headspace, I invite you to go through the Learner Experience Empathy Exercise.

LEARNER EXPERIENCE EMPATHY EXERCISE

Think back to your own experiences as a learner in any context, whether it was in school, at work, or in some other capacity.

Recall your BEST experience as a learner.

What was the situation and context?

What did you learn?

What did you see, hear and feel?

What were the conditions that made this the best experience for you as a learner?

Write it all down.

Now, recall your WORST experience as a learner.

What was the situation and context?

What did you learn?

What did you see, hear and feel?

What were the conditions that made this the worst experience for you as a learner?

Write it all down.

Common themes across leaner experiences

Now that you've empathized with learners by recalling your own personal best and worst experiences as a learner, reflect on the reasons behind why you identified these two distinct experiences. While every learner is different, I believe that every person wants to have learning experiences that are impactful, memorable, and dare I say it, fun. I've done this contrasting exercise in many group settings over time and the emerging themes are strikingly similar. Feel free to compare with your personal reflections.

I'll start with the best experiences. The best experiences people recall are those whereby learners felt like they learned in ways that made them more competent to do their jobs and when the training was both a valuable use of their time and directly applicable to the work they needed to do. Some other words used to describe their best training experiences: "Personal, quality, took time for me, experience, empathy, kindness, valuable, learning, important, powerful, applicable, made sense."

Common themes from the best learning experiences:

1. Valuable use of learner's time

2. Increased learner's competence to do work/tasks

3. Directly transferrable and applicable to the learner's work/tasks

4. Pleasant/positive overall experience

The worst experiences people recall are those whereby learners did not feel supported during training or on the job, like the company was not prepared for their arrival when the employee started the new job and training, and when the individual did not feel adequately equipped to effectively perform job duties. Some other words used to describe their worst training experiences: "Waste of time, frustrating, rushed, impersonal, impatient trainer, too much information at once, choppy, disorganized, irrelevant."

Common themes from the worst learning experiences:

1. Lack of support to learner during training or on the job
2. Learner perceptions that company was unprepared
3. Learner did not feel equipped to effectively perform work/tasks
4. Unpleasant/negative overall experience

These common themes are not entirely surprising. According to adult learning theory (Knowles, 1990), adult learners need to know why they are learning something and how to apply what is covered in the learning experience directly in their jobs. Therefore, in order to ensure an optimal learning experience, it would behoove us as practitioners to uphold a learner-centric mindset.

Curators aren't just for museums

In order to truly embody what it means to be a learner-centric learning and development practitioner, we must adopt the role and mindset of a learning experience curator, fundamentally believing that best practices from creating incredible customer experiences (i.e. Nordstrom) should be translated and applied to the learner experience.

I use the word "curator" very intentionally because we do not just design and deliver training programs. Think about the role of museum or gallery curators. They manage entire collections of art and artifacts, design displays and exhibitions, and provide information. They attend to various works of art and make careful selections of pieces that move, educate, and impact the public and museum visitors from all walks of life. As learning experience curators, when we design and deliver training programs, we draw from our endless vessels of intellect and knowledge to carefully craft an overall learning experience.

While we have our clients who we contract with, the ones who "pay us" to design, deliver, and evaluate training programs, we never forget about the end recipients of the training programs we create: our learners. We strive to find harmony across various stakeholders so that we can design optimized learning programs that are memorable, impactful, and high-touch. We leave our learners equipped to do their best work and thinking, "Wow, that was the best experience ever!" We leave our clients thinking, "Wow, that was so worth it and I can't wait to work with them again!"

Our mission is to add value to organizations with high-impact training programs by curating world-class learning and development experiences.

We are learning experience curators.

Chapter 2

My 7-Step Process
for High-Impact Training

Why did I create my own process?

Many of my clients, peers, and colleagues have always been saying that they wish they could do what I do when it comes to creating learning programs. My process is practical, user-friendly, replicable, flexible and fast. Most importantly, it enables learning practitioners to demonstrate value to both the client and the learners! I have chosen to document and share my 7-step process because I believe that until now, there has not been a field book like this that practitioners can flip to over and over again when creating training programs.

I am well aware that there are popular models like ADDIE (Analysis, Design, Develop, Implement, Evaluate) and SAM (Successive Approximation Model). While they are excellent in their own rights for designing learning solutions, I have heard from practitioners that they are difficult to apply in practice because organizations move very quickly. Unfortunately, I find that it has become too common that by the time people solicit the help of learning practitioners, the need for training is more reactive rather than proactive. This limits the amount of time a learning practitioner can thoroughly utilize and apply a comprehensiveness model.

In my experience designing 50+ learning programs throughout my career, it pains me to say that I have not once been able to fully execute against a model. Yes, I have referred to models to help guide me, but found that I needed to create my own process that I could apply and replicate in practice. I have come up with a process that has worked for me and I have been able to refine it throughout the years.

My 7-step process

My process for high-impact training covers the different touch points you will have with your client throughout the duration of a training project. It has enabled me to create training sessions in record time (as quickly as one week!) as well as designing full-scale, year-long programs. My process contains seven stages that you can customize to the timeline that you agree upon with your client. The timeline will vary depending on your client's needs such as program scale, sense of urgency with implementation, and client readiness.

Tadjbakhsh's 7-Step Process for High-Impact Training:

1. Client Intake
2. Learner Inquiry
3. Analysis and Insights
4. Learning Objective and Success Metrics
5. Session Blueprint
6. Program Deliverables
7. Training Launch and Follow Up

The forthcoming chapters go into depth about each of the seven steps with practical tools and templates that I hope you will find yourself referring to over and over again.

How to use this book

This book is for learning practitioners who need to create training sessions from scratch and want to do it in the most efficient and effective way to produce high-impact training. Each chapter provides context and details for each stage in my 7-Step Process for High-Impact Training. At the end of each chapter, you will find the corresponding tools and templates. Additionally, a complete packaging of the tools and templates can be found in sequential order in the Learning and Development in Practice Toolkit at the end of the book.

If this is your first time creating a training program, I highly recommend reading this book from start to finish. Better yet, find yourself a client so that you can apply and utilize the tools and templates as you go. Once you finish the book and start to work with more and more clients, flip to the relevant sections of this book as you partner with each client so that you can always ensure that you are adding value to organizations with high-impact training programs.

Good luck and have fun curating unforgettable learning and development experiences!

Chapter 3

Client Intake

Throughout the duration of your client engagement, remember that it is all about being high-touch. A client is someone with whom you've already contracted, which means that they are investing in your time and talents to help them solve a problem, whether that be you working as an internal or external practitioner. Ask yourself: "How can I do everything in MY control to ensure that my client has the best experience ever with me? How can I add value in every interaction with my client so that they never feel like they need to question the return on their investment in me?" Always add value in every interaction and make every effort to ensure that each interaction is pleasant.

You are not just a consultant performing a series of tasks. You are in the business of service and hospitality because you are SERVING your client. Adopting this mentality will not only make you stand out from all other practitioners and consultants, but it will also show your client that you are dedicated to and invested in your client's success. After all, your success is a direct reflection of your client's success. Moreover, adopting and committing to this mindset will build your reputation as a valued partner, which will lead to consistent repeat business and referrals.

The client intake meeting is where you get to set the stage and demonstrate how you will show up for your client throughout the duration of the project - always going above and beyond. It is important to have a client intake meeting at the start of a new training project. This is the first formal meeting and acts as the initial touch point to reassure your client that they made the right decision to work with you. You will reassure your client of this with your presence and actions right away during the client intake meeting so that your client can immediately begin to see a return on the investment they made in you.

Scheduling a client intake meeting

An intake meeting can be in person or virtual; use good judgment and do what you believe will allow you to best serve your client. Some clients prefer to meet and connect virtually while others prefer in-person. I always like to have the first meeting in person unless if there are geographical restrictions. In my experience, meeting in person, especially with new clients, leaves a personal and lasting positive impression.

If you are an external practitioner, you will have contracted with the client prior to having a formal client intake meeting. If you are an internal practitioner, you will want to partner with your client to schedule time for a formal client intake meeting. The purpose of the client intake meeting is to ensure that both you and your client are on the same page for the training project. The Client Intake Meeting Guide can be used to help you prepare for your client intake meeting.

There will be times when a client will reach out to you for a quick, informal and impromptu intake because they have a problem they need you to help solve with a training solution. If this happens, which can be quite often especially for internal practitioners, respectfully listen to the client so that they feel heard because this will build your rapport with the client. However, be sure to ultimately refrain from making any promises on delivering any solutions and having this impromptu conversation act as a client intake meeting. You cannot serve your client well with an impromptu discussion. Above all, making promises to deliver solely from an impromptu "intake" may result in your time being wasted because while your client expressed energy about enlisting your help in the impromptu conversation, they may not be ultimately committed to partnering with you over time in the ways you need them to in order to see the training project through to completion.

In sum, if you are in this situation: listen to the client, make them feel heard, and close the conversation with the next step that you will propose some time on their calendar for a follow-up discussion to better understand their needs and review a project timeline. If you hear back, this is great because now you can adequately prepare for the client intake meeting. If you do not hear back from them, that's okay too - the client may not have been able or ready to fully commit quite yet. Shoot them a follow-up email in approximately 6-8 weeks to show that you want to help and will be happy to do so when they are ready.

Preparing for a client intake meeting

Before you meet with your client, you should do some pre-meeting preparation so that you can make the best of both your time and your client's time. The purpose of the client intake meeting is to ensure that both you and your client are on the same page for the training project. You want to understand the purpose and desired outcomes of the training, remind the client about the timeline and deliverables, and establish clear next steps. See the Client Intake Meeting Checklist, Client Intake Confirmation Template, and Client Intake Meeting Guide to help you get ready for your client intake meeting.

Your goals for a client intake meeting

You have three goals you want to achieve as a result of the client intake meeting:

1. Understand the purpose and desired outcomes of the training from the client's perspective

2. Manage expectations on the training project timeline and deliverables

3. Establish clear next steps and ownership of action items

Understanding the purpose and desired outcomes of the training from the client's perspective

It is important that by the end of the client intake meeting, you fully understand your client's vision and desired outcomes of the training so that you can establish next steps with the client and align on a timeline for the project's duration. You want to understand your client's needs and desired outcomes not just from a training perspective, but also their broader vision. Draw out the purpose and desired outcomes of the training from your client's perspective so that you can understand what your client's ultimate vision and goals are with the training. You want to look beyond the training needs and understand your client's vision so that you can determine how you play an integral role in helping your client achieve the vision. Moreover, this allows you to connect with your client on a deeper level to learn what is truly important to them. You will save yourself a lot of time and energy upfront by doing this in the beginning because you want to manage expectations and also let your client truly see that you want to help them achieve their aspirations. Whether you are working as an internal or external practitioner, you need to understand your client's vision and what they want to achieve.

Let me give you an example of a situation when the training deliverable was rudimentary but made a big impact. I once worked with a CEO of a firm that wanted to make the basics in new hire training more scalable for their salespeople (e.g. how-to videos). With the CEO being the owner of his own small company, this meant that he was spending a lot more time than he wanted to training people on repetitive, mundane topics rather than using that time to mentor new employees during their on-the-job experiences. The CEO's vision was to spend his time at work adding value as a leader in ways that helped his employees grow and develop professionally, and he simply did not feel that he would be at his best to do this if he had to spend another minute re-explaining to employees how to input customer information into the database.

The gap here was that new employees did not know how to enter the data into the database, and of course, basic adult learning principles tell us that showing someone how to do something *once* does not result in long-term recall of the information. I worked with this CEO to outline the process for inputting customer data into the database so that employees knew exactly when customer data needed to go into the database. Once I understood the process and gathered the information needed for the tasks that would free up the CEO's time, I extracted the most important pieces that would help solve both the client and learners' problems. The final training deliverables were screen-capture videos and job aids on how to complete these tasks. This resulted in employees having on-demand learning for how to complete these basic tasks and the CEO achieving his vision of having more free time to do what gave him meaning and purpose: showing up as the leader he wanted to be for his team.

Meeting the client where they're at

During the client meeting, you must be present, remain curious, and actively listen. Your client should spend most of the time talking. Suspend judgment and refrain from jumping to brainstorming solutions with your client. Be committed to understanding your client's needs. Remember, you are there to serve them. Use the agenda and questions you prepared using the Client Intake Meeting Guide to stay on track.

Keep in mind that sometimes you will need to meet your clients where they are at. Some clients will be extremely open to your ideas for training solutions while others will be very specific and particular about the type of training they want. There will be times when in your heart, you know that what the client wants as the training solution will not solve their problems. In fact, you might know exactly what the solution is, but your client may not want to hear it or be ready to hear it. Use your best judgment in these situations as to what will best serve your client both now and long-term.

Sometimes during the client intake meeting, your client will give you the general specifications, or "specs," of the training. For example, a client might say: "I need a training on change leadership for my middle managers. It should be 60-90 minutes. I want to have 2-3 in-person sessions with approximately 20 people per session. I want to have the sessions next month."

Other times, the client will not provide any specs or information. This could be due to a number of reasons, whether it be because they are the messenger telling you because their boss wants to host the training or because they simply just do not know what they want or need. It is your job to help draw out the specs from your client so that you can have baseline information about their expectations. This will not only help you ensure that you are aligned with their expectations but also get a feel for their flexibility.

If you are ever stuck during the client intake meeting, this is your go-to question:

What do you want learners to walk away with by the end of the session?

The way to stay focused is to ask your client point blank what they want people to walk away with by the end of the training.

Based on what your client says for what they want people to walk away with by the end of the training, you can begin to capture or start thinking about evaluation methods by asking the client what results they want to see as a result of the training:

What do you want learners to <u>do</u> after the session both short-term and long-term as a result of the learning experience?

Asking this question about what the client wants learners to be able to do both short-term and long-term will help you clarify learning objectives for the training session.

Finally, ask what results would indicate that the training is successful:

What are the desired outcomes that would indicate to you that the training was successful?

Asking this question about the desired outcomes that would indicate that the training was successful is another way to align with the client, manage expectations and be results-driven.

Managing expectations on the training project timeline and deliverables

You have probably heard the popular adage commonly attributed to Benjamin Franklin: "If you fail to plan, you are planning to fail." For those of you who like metaphors, if you have an interview at a company's office that you've never visited, you would not just get into your car and drive aimlessly the day of the interview and hope to reach your destination "at some point." You would probably look up the address the night before to plan by what time you need to leave in order to get there approximately 10 minutes before your interview time. Perhaps you would even bake in an extra 5 minutes just in case if you hit unexpected traffic. From there, you would determine what time you need to start getting ready so that you know to leave on time.

Similarly, it is important to create a roadmap or project plan for your training project so that you can manage expectations with your client on the project's timeline and deliverables. The best way to do this is to start with the end in mind. Ask your client what the target launch date is for the program or training session. Depending on the program or session's complexity and your level of skill, you can set deadlines and create a project timeline. It is during the client intake meeting when you can negotiate with the client if the training launch date is unrealistic or unfeasible. You should always try to lean more towards the conservative side when creating a project timeline so that you can account for unexpected roadblocks.

A Training Roadmap is a helpful tool you can use during the intake meeting in order to align with your client on the project timeline and manage expectations. For example, in the Example Training Roadmap, my client intake is approximately two months prior to when the client wants to host the training session. I learn in the client intake meeting that the client wants to launch the training session in two months. I work backwards to create a timeline and bake in extra time as a buffer.

Example Training Roadmap

MON	TUE	WED	THUR	FRI
	Client Intake	Create Project Roadmap	Learner Inquiry	Learner Inquiry
Learner Inquiry	Learner Inquiry	Learner Inquiry	Analysis & Insights	Analysis & Insights
Analysis & Insights	Analysis & Insights	Analysis & Insights	Learning Objectives & Success Metrics	Learning Objectives & Success Metrics
Learning Objectives & Success Metrics	Learning Objectives & Success Metrics	Learning Objectives & Success Metrics	Learning Objectives & Success Metrics	Session Blueprint
Session Blueprint	Session Blueprint	Session Blueprint	Session Blueprint	Client Check-In
Program Deliverables	Program Deliverables	Program Deliverables	Program Deliverables	Program Deliverables
Program Deliverables	Client Check-In	Program Deliverables	Program Deliverables	Program Deliverables
	Training Launch			Client Follow-Up
Ongoing Follow-Ups as Needed				

Establishing clear next steps and ownership of action items

In order to ensure that the training project gains momentum, it is critical to establish next steps with your client. Make it clear about who owns which action items, whether that be you or your client. Make an attempt to schedule 3-5 learner interviews (more on this when we get to Learner Inquiry) at the end of the client meeting while you already have your client's attention so that you can get those locked into everyone's calendars. After the conclusion of your client intake meeting, send a follow-up email to your client within the next 24 hours containing the main points of the meeting and next steps. Use the Client Intake Follow-Up Email Template to help you draft your follow-up email.

Example

I will refer to this same change example throughout the book. I once worked with a client that wanted me to partner with them to create a training session for people leaders focused on leading through times of change. There was a large change coming that would significantly impact everyone's jobs, so my client needed managers to walk away with the skills that would enable managers to have open dialogue with their teams when introducing a large-scale change and ease the fear that team members would be feeling. The client wanted the session to be 60 minutes long and to roll out the training approximately five weeks after our client intake meeting to coincide with when the large change would be announced.

I will continue to refer to this example throughout the book when sharing templates.

Client Intake Meeting Checklist

Before the meeting

1. Email the client at least 48 hours prior to the meeting to confirm the date and time of your meeting. Confirm meeting address (in-person) or phone number/link (virtual) in your email.

   a. *See Client Intake Confirmation Template.*

2. Prepare an agenda and questions for the client intake meeting.

   a. *See Client Intake Meeting Guide.*

   b. *See Client Intake Meeting Question Bank.*

3. Prepare a training project roadmap with your standard/preferred timeline as a baseline.

   a. *See Example Training Roadmap.*

4. Ensure that you have all documents and note-taking materials handy.

5. Take a deep breath, smile, be pleasant and get excited! You are going to help make your client's life better by adding value right away!

During the meeting

1. Utilize your agenda and questions to stay on track.

2. Understand the purpose and desired outcomes of the training from the client's perspective.

3. Manage expectations on the training project timeline and deliverables.

4. Establish clear next steps and ownership of action items.

5. Make an attempt to schedule 3-5 learner interviews.

After the meeting

1. Email the client within the next 24 hours (*see Client Intake Follow-Up Email Template*):

   a. Summarize the main points and training roadmap with due dates for key deliverables.

   b. Provide an outline of next steps.

   c. Confirm dates, times, and locations of upcoming learner interviews.

2. Follow up with the client as needed.

Client Intake Confirmation Template

In-Person Meeting – Email Confirmation Template:

Hi [Client's Name],

I hope all is well! I am looking forward to our meeting this [day of week], [date], [time] at [location/address].

Please do not hesitate to contact me if you need anything. Thank you and I hope you have a wonderful day!

See you soon,
[your name]
[best number to get in contact with you]

Phone Meeting – Email Confirmation Template:

Hi [Client's Name],

I hope all is well! I am looking forward to our call this [day of week], [date] at [time]. I will call you at [client's phone number].

Please do not hesitate to contact me if you need anything. Thank you and I hope you have a wonderful day!

Talk soon,
[your name]
[best number to get in contact with you]

Virtual Meeting – Email Confirmation Template:

Hi [Client's Name],

I hope all is well! I look forward to connecting with you this [day of week], [date], [time]. Details for joining the meeting can be found below.

[virtual meeting link/joining details]

Thank you and please do not hesitate to contact me if you need anything. I hope you have a wonderful day!

Talk soon,
[your name]
[best number to get in contact with you]

Client Intake Meeting Guide

Meeting Agenda Template

Topic	Objective	Time
Welcome & Introduction	• Ask client how they're doing and "what's new" in their world to build rapport. • Introduce yourself and briefly summarize your credentials to build credibility. • State the purpose of the call. Review the agenda you prepared and what you hope to accomplish in the meeting. Ask client if it sounds like a good plan and if they have any questions.	3-5 minutes
Discovery	• Understand the purpose and desired outcomes of the training from the client's perspective. Try to uncover the problem they need help solving. • Ask the questions you prepared for the meeting (use Question Bank to prepare). Have an open dialogue.	30-35 minutes
Expectations	• Establish how you and the client will work together. • Manage expectations with the training project timeline by reviewing the Training Roadmap. • Achieve consensus on deadlines for key deliverables and activities. • Ask the client if they have any questions.	7-10 minutes

Closing & Next Steps	• Establish clear next steps and ownership of action items.	5-10 minutes
	• Make an attempt to schedule 3-5 learner interviews.	
	• Inform the client that you will email them a summary of the meeting's main points, their customized training roadmap, an outline of key next steps, and confirmation of upcoming learner interviews.	
	• Ask the client if they have any additional questions or if there is anything else they would like to discuss.	

Client Intake Meeting Question Bank

Note: Questions are <u>not</u> listed in a preferred sequential order. Select the questions that will help you optimize your time with your client during the intake meeting. Modify and/or write your own questions accordingly. Bolded questions are highly recommended.

- What is the problem you are hoping to solve with training?
- Why do you believe training is part of the solution to the problem? Could there be other potential solutions that you have not yet explored or thought of as options?
- How will you, your team, and/or your organization benefit from solving this problem?
- What are the gaps between your current and ideal situation? What are the roadblocks?
- **What do you want learners to walk away with (learn) by the end of the session?**
- **What do you want learners to <u>do</u> after the session both short-term and long-term as a result of the learning experience?**
- **What are the desired outcomes that would indicate to you that the training was successful?**
- Who is the audience (learners) that will participate in the training?
  a. Demographics, number of people, job titles, locations, languages, educational background, characteristics, pain points, etc.
- How would you describe the learning culture of the organization (or culture in general)?
- How will learners be supported to sustain behaviors they learn as a result of the training?
- When are you looking to launch/host the training session(s)?

- How do you envision the training to be rolled out?
- Do you have a preference for the modality in which the training is delivered, e.g. in-person, virtual, or something else?
- What else would you like to share that we have not yet had a chance to talk about?

Client Intake Follow-Up Email Template

Hi [Client's Name],

I enjoyed connecting with you today! I am excited for our partnership and helping you launch [training topic/name] on [launch date]. As promised, I have enclosed our training roadmap which outlines key milestones, deadlines, and deliverables.

Here are the main points we covered:

- [business case + problem to be solved with training]
- [training audience/learner population]
- [what learners should walk away with/learn by the end of the training]
- [desired short-term and long-term learner behaviors as a result of training]
- [desired outcomes that indicate training was successful]

The next step is for me to conduct a series of interviews with 3-5 people from the training audience so that I can analyze and extract insights that will maximize the impact of the training in a customized, meaningful way for your employees. We confirmed the following:

- [Interview 1 date, time, location, etc.]
- [Interview 2 date, time, location, etc.]
- [Interview 3 date, time, location, etc.]

Once I complete the learner interviews and my analysis, I will prepare a training strategy for us to review the week of [date]. Please do not hesitate to contact me at any time.

Thank you very much and I hope you have a wonderful day! Talk soon.

Regards,
[your name]
[best number to get in contact with you]

Chapter 4

Learner Inquiry

One of the biggest, and sadly, most common mistakes I see happen after a client intake meeting is that practitioners jump straight into training design. No inquiry, no strategy, no plan, but fast-tracking to training design. This is a careless yet sadly, common mistake because practitioners want to get to work quickly to produce training content. This NEEDS to stop! It not only diminishes our ability to make an impact in organizations but also makes us look lazy.

As tempting as it is, do NOT get caught up in trying to jump immediately into creating content for the training session. Before even THINKING about designing any program deliverables, we must conduct learner inquiry, complete analyses and extract insights, compose learning objectives and success metrics, and draft a training blueprint, respectively. All of these are covered in the forthcoming chapters. In this chapter, we focus on learner inquiry.

Learner Inquiry consists of three components:

1. Writing the problem from the learner's perspective.

2. Constructing a hypothesis for how you believe the problem can be solved.

3. Testing your hypothesis by engaging with the select individuals in the learner population (training audience).

Writing the problem from the learner's perspective

Our mission is to add value to organizations with high-impact training programs by curating world-class learning and development experiences. We add value by solving our client's needs, and we solve our client's needs by understanding and solving our learners' problems. Problems are everywhere and opportunities are everywhere. It is our job to find problems and opportunities.

When meeting with your client, what were they complaining about? What were your assumptions? How do these translate to what problems learners are facing, your proposed solution, and what can be covered in the training session to help solve these problems? This first step after you learn about what your client envisions for the training during the client intake meeting is to take some time to reflect and rewrite the problem from the perspective of the learner. In other words, reframe the problem from the perspective of the learner.

You need to define the problem(s) from the learner perspective because learners are the end recipients of your training session. If you don't try to empathize and make an attempt to understand what problems they might be facing, it diminishes your ability to get through to them and deliver the best possible training session. Furthermore, framing the problem from the learner perspective helps you as a practitioner narrow down on focus areas for the training session's content. Your training session will be more impactful because you will be able to deliver with content that will help solve the problems your learners are having.

Learner Problem Framework

In order to reframe and write the problem from the learner's perspective, fill in the brackets in the following sentence as if you are one of your learners:

I need a way to [learner's need] because [insight].

Reframing the problem like this builds your empathy as a practitioner and will remind you what you ultimately want to solve for. The learner problem should always be written from a learner perspective.

Learner Problems Template and Example

Below I use the learner problem template to write the problem from the learner's perspective with the change leadership example I introduced at the end of chapter three. In the client intake meeting, my client stated that they needed managers to walk away with skills that would enable them to have open dialogue with their teams so that they can help ease the fears of their team members during times of change.

Template	Example
I need a way to [learner's need] because [insight].	I need a way to have open and productive dialogue with my team members so that I can help them feel more at ease during stressful times full of change.

Once you believe that you understand the problem(s) from the learner's perspective, you will then write your proposed solution to the problem by constructing a hypothesis.

Constructing a hypothesis for possible solutions

Once you write the problem from a learner perspective, you then need to construct a hypothesis about what you believe will solve the learner problem(s). In order to do this, you need to think about what you can do with training to address the problem. Your hypothesis is an expectation of learner behavior given a specific condition. Do not spend too much time trying to perfect your words for the learner problem(s) and hypothesized solution(s). Once you write them, these are not yet set in stone. Rather, these are *proposed* solutions that you will *test* during learner interviews.

Hypothesized Solution Framework

In order to construct a hypothesized solution as to what you think will solve the learner problem(s), fill in the brackets in the following sentence:

By [doing something/creating a type of experience], then [this outcome].

This step is just as critical as writing the problem from the learner's perspective because your hypothesis will help you stay on track to solve the right problem(s) for the learner. You want to do it side-by-side with the learner problem(s) so that you have your thoughts organized.

Learner Problem Template	Hypothesized Solution Template
I need a way to [learner's need] because [insight].	By [doing something/creating a type of experience], then [this outcome].

Hypothesized Solutions Example

I use the hypothesized solution framework to construct a hypothesis with the change leadership example to which I have been referring.

Learner Problem	Hypothesized Solution
I need a way to have open and productive dialogue with my team members so that I can help them feel more at ease during stressful times full of change.	By improving leaders' coaching skills, leaders will have more productive dialogue with team members, especially during times of change.

Testing your hypothesis

Once you have posed the problem from the learner's perspective and proposed a hypothesized solution, it is time to test your hypothesis. Testing your hypothesis enables you to maximize the impact of your training by ensuring that you are using training to solve the right learner problems. Moreover, you are NOT your learner. Testing your hypothesis helps you get to know your learner so that you can improve the relevance and viability of the training.

There are varying methods you can use to test your hypothesis, such as observation, questionnaires, interviews, focus groups, collaboration tools, records, documents, historical data, and more (Noe, 2017). My preference is to conduct learner interviews because I can execute them rather quickly and simultaneously gather rich, informative data. I recommend conducting somewhere between three to five learner interviews or until you feel that you have enough information to move forward; aim for a minimum of three learner interviews.

Learner interviews

My goal with learner interviews is to better understand the existing behaviors of learners, identify their pain points, learn more about their goals and desires, and most importantly, uncover the truth! How painful is the learner problem? How many learners have this problem? What do the learners really need from a training session? How can I contribute in order to help solve the problem?

The purpose of interviews is NOT to find ways to validate our hypotheses. Interviews are <u>not</u> a way to build a case for what we want to do. While we prepare questions in advance for our interviews with learners, we must enter each interview with genuine curiosity and openness. If we go into the interview looking only for information that validates our assumptions, then we have failed. Our mission is to understand our learners' problems and how we can solve those problems with training.

Simple tips for formulating powerful interview questions

There are many books and tools dedicated specifically to asking powerful questions. In fact, there is a Right Question Institute focused on making it possible for all people to learn how to ask better questions! As an organizational psychologist, I have taken multiple intensive courses focused solely on research methods and asking questions. Please refer to the Preparing for Your Interviews worksheet I created to help you formulate your interview questions. Furthermore, I have outlined my distilled interview tips below that I have customized for application in the context of learner interviews:

- Interview questions should be hypothesis-based: Your mission is to find the truth about your learner's problems in relation to your client's needs and your proposed hypothesis. Make sure that your interview questions are based on your hypothesis.

- Ask open-ended questions: You want to get as much information as possible. Closed questions (usually start with "Do you" or "when" or "which" or "would") that result in the interviewee responding with a yes, no, or one-sentence answers do not lend themselves to opening up a dialogue. Open questions (usually start with "how" or "why") open up the conversation and prompt the interviewee to provide richer, more informational responses.

- ○ Closed question example: "Would you like to be able to improve your coaching skills?"

- ○ Reframed as an open question: "Can you tell me about how you like to coach your team members?"

- Avoid leading questions: Leading questions do not help you uncover the truth because they are biased towards helping you build a case for what you want to do. Be disciplined about keeping questions as neutral as possible so that you can learn more about the learner problems from varying perspectives.

  - ○ Leading question example: What are your frustrations with your company going through the current changes?

  - ○ Reframed as a neutral question: How do you feel about your company going through the current changes?

- Focus on individual instances: When you ask the learner to recall a specific instance, it allows you to tap into what they remember about the event and probe to learn about their distinct behaviors that occurred. When you focus on a topic more generally rather than an individual instance, you lose the salience of the learner's experience.

  - ○ General question example: What do you usually do to coach an employee who is disengaged?

  - ○ Reframed to have the learner recall an individual instance: What did you do the last time you had an employee on your team who completely disengaged?

- Learn about their current behaviors: Ask what learners are doing right now so that you can find out more about their current shortcuts and/or workarounds.

  - ○ Example: "What are you currently doing to motivate your team during the change?"

- Keep them talking: Ask clarifying questions and probe as needed to truly understand what your interviewees mean. Do not ever assume what they mean. If you ever find yourself making assumptions, drawing conclusions, or needing clarification, ask a probing question such as:
  - ○ "Can you tell me more about…"
  - ○ "In regards to what you said earlier about..."
  - ○ "What do you mean by..."
  - ○ "What does that look like?"

- Always end with this last question: "Is there anything else you want us to know?" This opens up the conversation for the learner to share whatever else has been on their mind that they have not yet had a chance to talk about during the interview. You will be surprised by how many additional insights you can extract from this final question.

Conducting the interview

When conducting learner interviews, you want to balance warmth and friendliness with professionalism. This will make the interviewees feel comfortable in terms of being at ease but also feeling safe to transparently share and be open with you.

After general introductions and greetings, you need to set the stage and open the interview. You want to tell the interviewee about the purpose of the interview and that you've prepared a list of questions you would like to cover. You also want to establish confidentiality when applicable, inform the interviewee that notes will be taken to capture key points, and ask if the interviewee has any questions before you begin. See the Learner Interview Guide for a general script that you can use and adapt. Be sure to pause throughout your opening so that it does not feel like a long-winded monologue. Make sure to close at the end of the interview by thanking the interviewee and sharing next steps as to what they can expect.

Note-taking during an interview

Personally, I type very fast, much faster compared to when I am writing things down with a pen, so you would think that I would bring my laptop to take notes during learner interviews. However, I find that having a laptop creates a physical barrier between the interviewee and me if I am the sole interviewer. It makes things less personal, more obstructive, and somewhat intimidating, so I always take handwritten notes when I am the sole interviewer. I write down my notes in bullet points to keep track of each thought or main point throughout the interview. It also makes it easier to review and process the notes later.

The best-case scenario is for there to be two people when conducting the interview so that one can focus solely on connecting with the interviewee, asking questions, actively listening, and probing accordingly while the second person takes notes on a laptop to capture everything. If you do go this route, make sure to introduce the note-taker so that it does not feel awkward. I personally like to take a moment to say, "This is [note-taker's name]. They are here today to help me take notes on their laptop throughout our conversation. Only [note-taker's name] and I will have access to these notes and will never share your name and responses, only general comments we have collected from all the people we interview." Give the note-taker an opportunity to say hello and make the interviewee feel comfortable. I sometimes like to make a joke to put the interviewee at ease by saying something like, "Don't mind [note-taker's name]'s furious typing. We just want to make sure that we are capturing what you say because your feedback is important and valuable."

Worksheet: Preparing for Your Interviews

Use this worksheet to prepare questions for your learner interviews. You can transfer them into your Learner Interview Guide once you've crafted your questions.

Learner Problem Template	Hypothesized Solution Template
I need a way to [learner's need] because [insight].	By [doing something/creating a type of experience], then [this outcome].

Interview Questions

Write down at least 5 interview questions that will help you test your hypothesis and learn more about your learner's pain points.

Interview Questions
[Question 1]
[Question 2]
[Question 3]
[Question 4]
[Question 5]

Learner Interview Guide

Use this template to prepare for your learner interviews. Print or save multiple versions so that you can use one for each interview. Be sure to adapt as needed and/or if there are multiple interviewers/ note-takers.

Opening

"Hello, [interviewee's name]! Thank you for taking the time to meet with me today. My name is [your name] and I am partnering with [client's name] on a training project. My goal for today is to learn about your experiences and perspective in relation to [topic] so that we can take action to [what you will do, e.g., "improve your experi-ence..."]. I have prepared a list of questions that I would love to cover, but really, today is about having more of a conversation. I am going to jot down some notes while we talk so that I make sure to capture your valuable insights. Also, I want to make sure you know that what you share with me today is completely confidential. This means that only I will have access to these notes and will never share your name and responses, only general comments I have collected from all the people I interview. With that being said, what questions do you have before we begin?"

Question	Interview Notes
[Question 1]	• [Note] • [Note]
[Question 2]	• [Note] • [Note]
[Question 3]	• [Note] • [Note]

[Question 4]	• [Note] • [Note]
[Question 5]	• [Note] • [Note]

Closing

"Great! Well, that brings us to the end of our discussion. I really appreciate you taking the time to meet with me today, [interviewee name]! In terms of next step, what you can expect is [next steps that are relevant to the learner]. Thank you again so much!"

Chapter 5

Analysis and Insights

Once you complete conducting your learner interviews, it is time to analyze your interview data, extract insights, make sense of some of your learners' underlying problems, and adjust your hypothesized solutions as needed.

I believe that Steve Jobs said it best: "Some people say 'give the customer what they want.' But that's not my approach. Our job is to figure out what they're going to want before they do. I think Henry Ford once said, 'If I'd asked customers what they wanted, they would have told me, 'A faster horse!'" People don't know what they want until you show it to them. That's why I never rely on market research. Our task is to read things that are not yet on the page."

The same goes for us as learning experience curators and practitioners. We use the learner interviews as a way to uncover the truth so that we can metaphorically "read things that are not yet on the page," or draw out the common themes from our learner interviews to help us modify our hypothesized solutions. By doing so, we are able to determine learning objectives and success metrics that incorporate the most relevant solutions to our learners' problems so that we can help our client achieve their desired outcomes.

Analyzing interview notes

Review each of your interview notes to look for key themes that emerged both within and across all of the interviews. I like to look at one individually and highlight key phrases. I try to look for learner high points or strengths as well as struggles, pain points, and barriers so that I can identify critical gaps that pertain to learning or performance, specifically focusing on key behaviors and strategies. For example, when analyzing the notes from my learner interviews for the change leadership training, I found that there was a huge gap with leaders not being able to remain calm and maintain their composure during times of change. This was because the change placed a lot of stress and pressure on the leaders in ways that they did not know how to self-manage or cope in a healthy way. I also noticed that leaders did not have tangible strategies, ideas, or tools they could implement to engage and motivate employees. They had the desire to do so but did not necessarily know how to do it. I also found confirmation of the leaders' coaching skills gap in terms of not being able to have productive dialogue with team members.

Generating actionable insights

Once you have uncovered emerging themes and gaps from analyzing your interview notes, it is time to extract those insights to make better sense of the learner problems and modify your hypothesized solution(s). You want to do two things before moving onto working on the learning objectives and success metrics (Chapter 6):

1. Modify the problems written from the learner's perspective.
2. Modify the hypothesized solutions for how you believe the problems can be solved.

Based on my analysis with the change leadership example, I was able to confirm the one problem I wrote from the learner's perspective. However, I also found two more that needed to be addressed in the training session. The first one in the table was the problem I wrote from the learner's perspective prior to conducting the learner interviews, while the last two were added after analyzing learner interview data.

Learner Problems
I need a way to have open and productive dialogue with my team members so that I can help them feel more at ease during stressful times full of change.
I need a way to remain calm & not lose my patience when I'm overwhelmed so that I can be a better leader for my employees.
I need a way to maintain employee motivation so that I can engage my team.

Next, I updated my hypothesized solutions for how I believed the learner problems could be solved with training. The first one in the table was from the learner's perspective prior to conducting the learner interviews, while the last two were added after analyzing learner interview data.

Learner Problem	Hypothesized Solution
I need a way to have open and productive dialogue with my team members so that I can help them feel more at ease during stressful times full of change.	By improving leaders' coaching skills, leaders will have more productive dialogue with team members, especially during times of change.
I need a way to remain calm and not lose my patience when I'm overwhelmed so that I can be a better leader for my employees.	By educating leaders on self-management best practices, leaders will remain calm, not lose their patience, and show up at their best during unprecedented times of change.
I need a way to maintain employee motivation so that I can engage my team.	By educating leaders on the basics of employee motivation and change management, leaders will better understand how people react to change and how to better motivate them.

Using this framework of learner problem and hypothesized solution sets you up to take action on the insights acquired from data analysis. This is because you are going to utilize the hypothesized solutions to inform your learning objectives and success metrics and training content.

Chapter 6

Learning Objectives and Success Metrics

Once you have finalized your learner problems and hypothesized solutions, it is time to start thinking about the learning objectives for your training and the success metrics you will use to evaluate the training. Learning objectives and success metrics strategically prepare you before you move onto creating your training blueprint and program deliverables (more on these in Chapters 7 and 8).

Learning Objectives

A learning objective is a statement that clearly illustrates the intended and desired outcome of the training. In order to construct learning objectives, you need to draw from the learner problems and hypothesized solutions. These will help to inform the training content for your session. Refer back to your finalized learner problems and hypothesized solutions to draft learning objectives. Translate the learner problems and hypothesized solutions into defined learning objectives, which will act as the desired outcomes of training. Use the Learning Objectives Worksheet to draw up your learning objectives.

Learning objectives should be specific, observable and measurable. Each learning objective must begin with a verb that outlines

an observable behavior, such as "employ, appl
assess, etc." I like to use Bloom's Taxonomy of
tives (Bloom, Engelhart, Furst, Hill, & Krathwoh
Taxonomy Revised (Anderson et al., 2001). Using s
and measurable verbs will not only make expecta
learner, but also continue to help you with prioritizir   .... ior the
training session.

Reference Material: List of Example Verbs in Bloom's Taxonomy Revised

Remembering	Recall, list, name, label, define, cite, recite, recognize
Understanding	Arrange, classify, convert, identify, explain, discuss, summarize, sort, describe
Applying	Apply, compute, demonstrate, establish, illustrate, implement, modify, predict, coordinate, employ, prepare, utilize
Analyzing	Analyze, determine, calculate, categorize, classify, contrast, critique, defend, detect, distinguish, examine
Evaluating	Assess, build, choose, compare, formulate, hypothesize, integrate, justify, judge, manage, prioritize, recommend, propose, synthesize
Creating	Adapt, anticipate, collaborate, combine, compose, communicate, create, design, facilitate, initiate, negotiate, perform, plan, resolve

arning Objectives Worksheet

Learner Problem	Hypothesized Solution	Learning Objective

Example Learning Objectives Worksheet

Learner Problem	Hypothesized Solution	Learning Objective
I need a way to have open and productive dialogue with my team members so that I can help them feel more at ease during stressful times full of change.	By improving leaders' coaching skills, leaders will have more productive dialogue with team members, especially during times of change.	Employ best practices for having more productive dialogue with team members and increasing team psychological safety.
I need a way to remain calm and not lose my patience when I'm overwhelmed so that I can be a better leader for my employees.	By educating leaders on self-management best practices, leaders will remain calm, not lose their patience, and show up at their best during unprecedented times of change.	Apply self-management best practices to reduce stress and increase patience during difficult situations.
I need a way to maintain employee motivation so that I can engage my team.	By educating leaders on the basics of employee motivation and change management, leaders will better understand how people react to change and how to better motivate them.	Assess and/or predict employee motivation; employ appropriate solution to increase motivation and engagement.

Success Metrics

"You can't fix what you don't measure." This is what one of my esteemed colleagues and organization development expert, Kathy Suarez, always says, and it has really stuck with me. It is especially relevant in the context of creating training programs. You need to establish what success looks like after you establish your learning objectives so that you have clear indicators that will let you know whether or not your training was an effective solution to your learners' problems, giving you focus and discipline. Moreover, metrics help you attain buy-in from your client.

You can have multiple success metrics for each learning objective. They should be a combination of measuring observable learner behaviors over time as well as other data points that evaluate transfer of training after you implement the training program. Outlining key metrics sets the stage for the direction of how your training makes an impact over a specific period of time and promotes long-term, sustainable behavior change. I recommend establishing a minimum of five success metrics to review at varying times:

1. Immediately after the training
2. 30 days post-training
3. Three months post-training
4. Six months post-training
5. One-year post-training

Do not confuse effort with results by focusing on vanity metrics that do not tell you anything about the effectiveness of the training! Vanity metrics can be learner attendance, surveys asking the learner about how helpful they found the training, or any other types of metrics that do not help you measure observed behaviors or desired outcomes. While learner satisfaction is important, you do not want to make that your focus. Just because learners enjoyed the training does not mean that they will change their behaviors or apply their learnings outside of the training session. You want to strike a balance between designing a world-class learning experience and promoting learning transfer beyond the training session. Therefore, declare success metrics that you can track over time to evaluate the effectiveness of your training. Make sure that your metrics are SMART: Specific, Measurable, Attainable, Realistic, and Time-bound (Locke & Latham, 1990). If you are feeling overly ambitious, you can create stretch goals, too.

Use the Success Metrics Worksheet to draft your metrics. Once you have finalized your learning objectives and success metrics, you may proceed to drafting your training session blueprint (see Chapter 7).

Success Metrics Worksheet

Learner Problem	Hypothesized Solution	Learning Objective

Success Metrics

Example Success Metrics Worksheet

Learner Problem	Hypothesized Solution	Learning Objective
I need a way to have open and productive dialogue with my team members so that I can help them feel more at ease during stressful times full of change.	By improving leaders' coaching skills, leaders will have more productive dialogue with team members, especially during times of change.	Employ best practices for having more productive dialogue with team members and increasing team psychological safety.
I need a way to remain calm and not lose my patience when I'm overwhelmed so that I can be a better leader for my employees.	By educating leaders on self-management best practices, leaders will remain calm, not lose their patience, and show up at their best during unprecedented times of change.	Apply self-management best practices to reduce stress and increase patience during difficult situations.
I need a way to maintain employee motivation so that I can engage my team.	By educating leaders on the basics of employee motivation and change management, leaders will better understand how people react to change and how to better motivate them.	Assess and/or predict employee motivation; employ appropriate solution to increase motivation and engagement.

Success Metrics

- Immediately post-training: Scores of 80% or better on post-training online quiz.

  o Quiz content: Blend knowledge/recall items and situational judgment items focused on productive dialogue, self-management, stress management, and employee motivation.

- 30/90/180/365 days post-training: Leadership pulse survey to learners' team members.

  o Measure leadership effectiveness via observed behaviors – increase by 10% at each time of measurement (stretch goal: 15%): Positive team climate, effective communication, self-management and composure, reactions under times of pressure.

  o Measure employee performance, engagement, motivation, and job satisfaction.

- 30/90/180/365 days post-training: Team member turnover decreases 10% at each time of measurement (stretch goal: 15%).

- 30/90/180/365 days post-training: Employee performance, engagement, motivation, and job satisfaction scores increase by 15% at each time of measurement (stretch goal: 20%).

Chapter 7

Session Blueprint

Once you have outlined your learning objectives and success metrics, it is time to move onto drafting your session blueprint. A training session blueprint is the skeleton of your training session that you plan out prior to designing any program deliverables. Depending on how hands-on your client is, you will want to check in with your client after creating the session blueprint in order to ensure that you have your client's buy-in to proceed with the design of program deliverables. See Client Check-In Deck Outline to help you create a presentation for the check-in meeting with your client. It is helpful to have a check-in with your client and present a high-level overview of the training session in case if they are not aligned to anything you propose. It is better to get the feedback early on rather than when it is cutting it too close to the training launch date. Moreover, checking in with your client builds your relationship with them and provides that high-touch level of service excellence.

Schedule your client check-in approximately one week in advance. Before scheduling the check-in, make sure that you have started and/or completed the majority of your session blueprint and client check-in deck. The session blueprint outlines your instructional flow, inclusive of every element in the training session. Take a look at one of my own session blueprints in the Session Blueprint Example to see how it can be helpful for you when you are getting ready to outline the session.

Be strategic and thoughtful about what you include in your session blueprint. Everything should always tie back to your learning objectives so that they solve the learners' problems and help your client achieve their desired outcomes. This is because if your client asks you why you decided to include specific elements in the training session (which they will), you will be adequately prepared to explain your rationale for including each and every element in the training. Use the check-in opportunity to gather early feedback from your client and get the green light to proceed. For example, this was when I explained to the client why it would be beneficial to increase the session length to 90 minutes. Listen to your client's feedback, answer their questions, and align on how you will incorporate the feedback when designing the program deliverables.

The session blueprint contains seven components:

1. Topic
2. What to cover
3. Learning objective
4. Delivery method
5. Materials
6. Facilitator (optional)
7. Time

Topic

"Topic" is the high-level subject you will be focusing on during that section of the training session. It should coincide with your training's purpose and learning objectives. For example, I have my topics as Welcome, The People Side of Change, Employee Motivation, Leader as Coach, Self-Management, and Close. It helps you look at the training from a high level when drafting and later reviewing your blueprint to make edits.

What to cover

"What to cover" includes the questions you will be answering with training content that your learner needs to know in order to achieve the learning objectives. "What to cover" helps you outline the flow of the training from the learners' perspective so that you make sure to address the common questions they would have during the training session. They help solve the learners' problems because you will be answering those questions in the training session in some fashion. For example, a lot of people might not have ever heard the term "self-management" before and how it relates to stress, so it would be important to cover the definition of self-management in the training, why it is particularly important during times of change, and best practices in self-management related to stress that increase leadership effectiveness.

Learning objective

Once you fill out "What to cover," copy and paste the corresponding learning objectives that coincide with what you will be covering under "Learning Objectives" in the session blueprint. The purpose of this exercise is to review "What to cover" once more after you add the learning objectives to see if what you will be covering indeed addresses your learning objectives. This part is extremely helpful because it allows you to see where you have added topics to cover that are not necessarily relevant to the learning objectives or have not fully included information in "What to cover" that will fully meet the learning objective. Do NOT just copy and paste the learning objectives and move on. Once you paste the learning objectives over into the session blueprint, go through each bullet-point under "What to cover" and ask yourself: "Does this help contribute to achieving the learning objective?" If not, remove it. Also ask yourself: "What am I missing that could inhibit me from helping my learners meet the learning objective?" Add bullet points accordingly.

Delivery method

"Delivery method" is where you will specify the type of activity that will be occurring during the learning session, whether that be instructor-led, small group discussion, large group discussion, an activity or something else. This column helps you see at a high level if you only have one type of delivery method. In order to keep learners engaged, consider mixing things up with varying delivery methods instead of just one. Refer back to best practices with adult learning principles and always remember that you are curating a learning experience! Ask yourself how you can make the training a high-impact, unforgettable learning experience that promotes transfer of training beyond the session.

Oftentimes, it will be tempting to become consumed with the intricacies when designing learning experiences: Immersive activities, cutting-edge techniques, new props and tools, unconventional room setups, etc. It will be tempting because this is the avenue for you to unleash your creativity and brilliance. However, you must constantly be reminding yourself that your learners are number one. They are the ones that must remain top of mind. This isn't the "you" show. This is a show you are putting on for the benefit of your learners. Your creativity and brilliance in your learning experiences will mean nothing if they do not, ultimately, add value.

I have seen it happen many times and I have done it myself too. We get excited about doing a certain type of activity in a training program and it becomes all-consuming. We try to force an activity into our session because it is profound or fun or powerful, but we know deep down that it does not make any sense to include it because it does not align with the learning objectives. This does not mean your idea is bad and that you should forget about it completely, but rather, that the idea is not relevant to this specific client and learners.

When you have these moments, write down those creative ideas and store them someplace easily accessible (I use Excel), describing the activity and in what types of situations it could work. This way, you become unattached to the idea and forcing it into training programs when it will not have maximum impact. Simultaneously, you begin to make your own "activity repository" over time full of your original and creative ideas that you can use with future clients when appropriate.

Make no mistake. I am in no way saying that you should bury your creativity when developing training programs. On the contrary, you should stretch yourself to be as creative as possible in ways that align with your program's learning objectives. What has made me successful and well known as a learning practitioner is inserting the wackiest, most creative, and unconventional activities perfectly in the contexts and situations where they belong...when they add the most value because of their relevance and translatability on the job. We add the most value when we are focused on ensuring that the components and delivery methods of our training programs align perfectly with the learning objectives.

Materials

"Materials" is where you capture whatever documents or materials you will need during each section of the training. "Materials" can include things like PowerPoint presentation, participant handout, number of flip charts, number of flip chart markers and how many of each color, pads of sticky notes, projector and screen, etc. The purpose of this column is for you to create a checklist of all the materials you will need throughout the session so that you can prepare your materials in advance of the session and ensure that you do not forget any critical items.

Facilitator

"Facilitator" includes the name(s) of the individuals who will be speaking and engaging with the training audience for the corresponding sections in the training. Sometimes, it might just be one person so that column will not always be needed. Other times when there are multiple facilitators whereby sections are broken up and/or assigned to specific facilitators, this column is important so that you can ensure proper prior preparation and smooth transitions from one facilitator to the next.

Time

"Time" is the number of minutes that will be spent on the corresponding sections of each training topic. This will help you outline how much time you want to spend on each topic. Always create buffers (approximately 3-5 minutes) in case some sections take longer than others.

Once you have received the green light from your client to proceed with designing training program deliverables, proceed to Chapter 8 to learn about creating program deliverables.

Session Blueprint Template

Topic	What to Cover	Learning Objective	Delivery Method	Materials	Facilitator	Time

Session Blueprint Example

Notes:

- Facilitator column was omitted because the facilitator was the same throughout the entire session.

- Materials column was omitted because the materials were the same throughout the entire session: PowerPoint Presentation and Participant Workbook.

Change Leadership Training Session Blueprint

Topic	What to Cover	Learning Objective	Delivery Method	Time
Welcome	• Why we're here • Learning objectives • Ground rules		• Instructor-led	3-5 min
The People Side of Change	• Context-setting • The impact of change & a leader's role • How can leaders partner with employees during change		• Instructor-led	5 min
Employee Motivation	• What is employee motivation • Why employee motivation is important • Leader's role in employee motivation	• Assess and/or predict employee motivation; employ appropriate solution to increase motivation and engagement	• Instructor-led • Independent activity • Small group discussion	25 min

Topic	What to Cover	Learning Objective	Delivery Method	Time
	• Present relevant/most frequent employee motivation tips/best practices • Leaders do an activity where they create a chart with each employee/team members, what motivates each of their team members, and action plan for moving forward – share in small groups			
Leader as Coach	• How to have productive dialogue with team members • Change management-type coaching conversations • Leaders do role play activity on having productive dialogue with team members	• Employ best practices for having more productive dialogue with team members and increasing team psychological safety.	• Instructor-led • Paired role play activity • Large group discussion	30 min

Topic	What to Cover	Learning Objective	Delivery Method	Time
Self-Management	• What is self-management • Why is self-management important during times of change • Present self-management best practices that will improve leadership effectiveness, reduce stress, and increase patience, specifically during times of change • Participants discuss which practices they want to apply/practice	• Apply self-management best practices to reduce stress and increase patience during difficult situations.	• Instructor-led • Small group discussion	15 min
Close	• Recap key points • Large group discussion about key takeaways • Participants share commitments to apply learnings from the session		• Instructor-led • Large group discussion	7-10 min

Client Check-In Deck Outline

Topic	What to Cover	Time
Title Slide	• Project title • Date of check-in	Less than 1 min
Project Purpose	• Business case • Client's current state vs. desired state • Client intake summary • Date of training launch	2 min
Training Project Roadmap	• Use image of Training Roadmap and a star/marker/color indicating: "We are here!" on Client Check-In box	2 min
Learner Insights	• Number of interviews conducted • Emerging themes • Final learner problems and hypothesized solutions side-by-side	2 min
Learning Objectives & Success Metrics	• Use highlights from "Success Metrics Worksheet" to create this slide • Ask for client's thoughts on if metrics/key results are realistic and feasible	4 min
Session Blueprint	• Use highlights from "Session Blueprint" to create this slide • Do not show every single detail, just the highlights UNLESS the client asks to see it	2 min

Feedback + Q&A	• Ask for the client's reactions and questions • Gather feedback and answer questions	10 min
Next Steps	• Align on updates that will be made to training • Align on next steps • Confirm training session logistics as needed (e.g., who will print materials, is the training room booked, what else is needed, etc.) • Schedule final pre-launch check-in call with client approximately one week prior to training launch	5-7 min

Chapter 8

Program Deliverables

I know you are probably anxious by now to start creating all of your training program materials. You are almost there. Before you open up a PowerPoint file and start creating the deck for your training session, you must know what content you are going to put into it! A good place to start is the content development matrix.

Content Development Matrix

The content development matrix is a critical tool for practitioners who need to develop training content and program deliverables but are not subject matter experts in the training topic(s) nor have immediate access to any subject matter experts. Most of us will not be subject matter experts in the training topics every single time we go to create training unless if it happens to be the same topic whenever we work with different clients. The content development matrix enables you to pull, document, and keep track of evidence-based information and best practices from various sources so that you can incorporate the relevant key points when developing your training content. This ensures that you are providing your learners with the most accurate, helpful, and up-to-date information related to the training topic. See the Content Development Matrix Template to start aggregating resources that you will use to develop your training session content.

Literature Review

The Literature Review is the top half of the content development matrix. This section is intended to help you find and critically assess articles, studies, and/or any other reputable sources that you could see yourself referring to in your training session. For example, I Googled thought leaders on employee motivation, coaching, and self-management for my change leadership session, looking for articles that helped answer the questions I had inputted into the "What to Cover" column of my training session blueprint. I found the original sources from which I annotated the purpose of the study/article, key findings and takeaways, strengths, limitations, and the best practices that I could apply in my change leadership training session.

I recommend finding references from diverse sources, such as top-tier I-O psychology journals (*Journal of Applied Psychology, Personnel Psychology, Academy of Management Journal, or Academy of Management Review*), textbooks, literature reviews from any journal, meta-analyses from any journal, or book summaries.

Application of findings from literature review

Once I felt like I had collected and reviewed enough sources (I recommend a minimum of five), I was ready to move to the bottom half of the content development matrix. This section is about translating what I had learned from my literature review into key principles that I would include in my training session, along with the learning objectives those principles meet.

Drafting program deliverables

I hope you appreciate and see how the session blueprint and content development matrix help keep you organized and focused prior to drafting any of your training program materials. In fact, they help make the design process easier because you have prepared all of your content up front.

While there are certainly a multitude of mediums you can utilize to design your training program, I focus primarily in this book on creating a training session PowerPoint deck with supplemental handouts. I have certainly used many different mediums, but PowerPoint decks have been the overwhelming majority, hence my focus on it in this book. Nevertheless, all of my steps up until now can be easily translatable to other training delivery methods other than PowerPoint.

Content before design!

After completing my content development matrix, I keep it handy along with my session blueprint while I open a new PowerPoint file to begin drafting the training deck. I transfer everything into the PowerPoint according to the session blueprint and content development matrix that I want to cover in the training session, whether it is content on a slide, in a handout, or in the facilitator notes. I transfer everything into the PowerPoint file slide-by-slide whereby each slide is a complete thought. See my example of one slide for the change leadership training, Training Session Slide Example: Draft State. Notice how there is no design elements...yet.

Once the content is in a good place, then you can seamlessly move to design. If the content is not there in ways that meet the learning objectives, then no amount of design will matter or make your intended impact. See the final state of the same slide from my change leadership training in my example, Training Session Slide Example: Final State. Notice how a lot of the notes that were on the slide in the draft state have now moved over to the presenter notes. I am still going to cover the content, I am just not going to have all those words on a slide because it is neither aesthetically appealing nor learner-friendly for a presentation.

When you finish designing the PowerPoint, move on to designing any session handouts or participant materials. For the change leadership training, I created a participant workbook so that learners could take notes, capture key points, and have on-demand access to their workbook by being able to take it away from the session. See an example page from the participant workbook that corresponds to the slide examples.

Finalizing program deliverables

With my 7-step process for high-impact training, you will most likely spend most of your time working on the session blueprint and content development matrix. If you did those two steps correctly, then designing program deliverables should be very smooth because you already did all of the hard work. The reason why Program Deliverables is the longest phase on the Training Roadmap is because design skill level varies by person. It also depends on the available resources you are able to tap into. I have had to be somewhat resourceful and teach myself design basics by primarily using shapes in PowerPoint to manipulate slide design and using sites that provide free stock images and icons. There are many resources out there that you can refer to if you want to learn more about the art and science of instructional design.

When you put the finishing touches on your program deliverables, you should ideally have one last check-in call with your client prior to training launch. This is not only to ensure that all logistics are good to go but it also is another touch point that creates that high-touch level of service to your client. Once you finish that check-in call with your client and everything is in order, it is time for you to prepare for show time - training launch time!

Content Development Matrix Template

Literature Review					
Article Title/ Citation	Purpose of the Study/ Article	Key Findings/ Takeaways	Strengths	Limitations	Application to Training Session
[Article 1]					
[Article 2]					
[Article 3]					
[Article 4]					
[Article 5]					

5+ key principles you will include in your training	Learning Objective

Training Session Slide Example: Draft State

Engaging & Motivating Employees During Change

- Set clear expectations and goals
  - Focus on getting your teams involved in the change
  - Be clear about how they contribute to the change
- Actively listen
  - Validate your employee's feelings by acknowledging fears and/or anger over the change – sometimes, people just want to feel heard
  - Create forums for open, honest, and two-way discussion
  - Listen to feedback and do your best to act on it
- Celebrate wins and milestones
  - Recognize people for the progress they are making to show people's contributions to the change
  - Create small, achievable milestones to increase feelings of accomplishment and sustain momentum

Training Session Slide Example: Final State

Engaging & Motivating Employees During Change

Slide time: 3 minutes

Now that we've talked about your role as a leader and how you can help your employees during this time of change, let's now dive deeper into how to engage and motivate employees during times of change

You want to set clear expectations and goals so that your team can have clarity and direction, especially during times of change when things can be ambiguous

- Focus on getting your teams involved in the change
- Be clear about how they contribute to the change

You want to also make sure that you actively listen by:

- Validating your employee's feelings by acknowledging fears and/or anger over the change – sometimes, people just want to feel heard
- Creating forums for open, honest, and two-way discussion
- Listening to feedback and doing your best to act on it

Lastly, it is absolutely critical to celebrate wins and milestones

- Recognize people for the progress they are making to show people's contributions to the change
- Create small, achievable milestones to increase feelings of accomplishment and sustain momentum

Transition to activity on the next slide.

Example Complementary Page from Participant Workbook

Engaging & Motivating Employees During Change

Set Clear Goals	_____
Actively Listen	_____
Celebrate Wins & Milestones	_____

Chapter 9

Training Launch and Follow-Up

I t's almost show time! Are you ready? Training launch is the day when you will deliver, deploy, or implement the training program. Training launches can be in-person, virtual, or multi-channel. You should be referring to your Training Roadmap that you created at the beginning of the project throughout all seven steps to prevent any surprises as it gets closer and closer to training launch.

One week before launch

Make sure you have one last check-in call with your client to ensure that everything is in order for the day of training launch. Express any concerns or risks that need to be mitigated as promptly as possible with the greatest sense of urgency. Use this check-in to also schedule a follow-up call with your client a few days after the training launch so that you can check in with the post-training delivery.

Find out during this call if the client wants to use their equipment or if you will be able to bring your own equipment (i.e. laptop). I cannot tell you how many times there have been issues with videos in Power-Point playing, the sound not working or the presentation system not working all together! Do everything you can to minimize stress the day of training launch. I would suggest trying to coordinate with your client that you arrive about one hour early so that you can test out the room and work with their tech/AV team to make sure that everything works if you are doing in-person delivery. For virtual delivery, definitely do a test run to ensure that people can access the virtual training space, can hear everything, and can see any materials that are being shared.

3-7 Days before launch

Check to make sure that all of your program deliverables are immaculate! No misspellings, no formatting gaffes, and no careless mistakes! I would recommend doing this the day after you finish everything so that you can see the deliverables with fresh eyes.

If you are the main facilitator, do several dry runs of your presentation and time yourself. Practice your "script" and make sure that you are not merely memorizing or reading words from a facilitator guide. That is not doing your learners justice. If you are feeling brave, record yourself on video so that you can see your mannerisms and correct anything that you want to adjust. I always try to get to know my content very well and go "off script" so that I do not have to worry so much about what I need to say when I am facilitating, but rather, focus on *how* I am going to say it and engage with learners throughout the session.

In terms of printing handouts and such, print one copy of all of your handouts first to make sure everything looks perfect. Ensure that the pages are flipping correctly if they are double-sided. Depending on if you are going to print everything or if your client is, do a test run first before sending everything to the printer.

Night before launch

Triple check to make sure that you have everything ready to go so that you do not forget anything the day of training launch.

Do you know which PowerPoint is the most recent version?

Did you print all the handouts?

Do you have your clicker?

Do you have your laptop charger?

Do you know the address and which conference room the training is in?

Day of launch

It is your time to shine and watch all your hard work come to fruition! Everything has prepared you for this moment! Your learners are your audience and you are the performer (if you are the facilitator, that is). Your mission is to provide the best possible experience to your learners in order to promote transfer of training, transform behavior, and add value to the organization.

You are completely relaxed because you have prepared for this day for a long time. You are ready! You are at the top of your game and you are going to make an impact with your learners today! Remember the number one thing: ensure an optimal experience for all learners.

Following up after training launch

You did it! Congratulations! You facilitated an incredible training launch. Just because the training session is over does not mean that the project has concluded. There is still work to be done. Connect with your client immediately after the training to gather their feedback and reactions. If your client did not attend the training, connect with them to let them know how it went. Confirm the date and time of your follow-up call as well while you have their attention and are excited to connect with them again.

Client follow up

During your client follow-up call, you want to gather feedback, conduct a retrospective so that you can iterate and improve the next training session or rollout when applicable, remind and touch base with the client about evaluating success metrics, inquire about the client's appetite for a sustainment plan, and establishing next steps. You want to ensure that the client feels like you delivered high-impact training and helped the client get closer to their desired state. It is important to urge the client to follow through on evaluating the success metrics so that they can track the impact of their investment in the training over time.

The Client Follow-Up Meeting Guide can be used to help you prepare for your client follow-up meeting.

Purpose of client follow-up call:

1. Gather feedback and opportunities for improvement with future training iterations

2. Touch base regarding evaluation of success metrics so that the client can optimize the return on their investment

3. Inquire about sustainment plans

4. Gauge the client's feelings and satisfaction with your services

5. Establish next steps

Be sure to follow up with your client and learners when you can.

Client Follow-Up Meeting Guide

Meeting Agenda Template

Topic	Objective	Time
Welcome	• Ask client how they're doing. • State the purpose of the call. Review the agenda you prepared and what you hope to accomplish in the meeting. Ask the client if it sounds like a good plan and if they have any questions.	2 min
Training Retrospective	• Ask for the client's reactions and what they have been hearing about the training session questions. • Ask for feedback: What went well, what could have been improved, and what were some areas of untapped potential to consider for future training iterations.	10-15 min
Success Metrics & Sustainment Planning	• Inquire about the client's plans for sustainment in order to promote training transfer. • Provide suggestions and weave in evaluating the success metrics so that the client can optimize the return on their investment. • Ask the client if they have any questions.	10-15 min
Client Satisfaction & Next Steps	• Ask the client what else there is that you can do to support them. Ask how they are feeling about the investment they made in the training.	7-10 min

- Ask the client if they have any additional questions or if there is anything else they would like to discuss.
- Establish next steps.

Conclusion

Congratulations! You now hold the keys to creating training programs that make an impact for individuals, organizations and beyond. I sincerely hope that you feel like this book equipped you with the skills and information to curate strategic, targeted, world-class learning and development experiences. I took great care myself in curating this book just for you, meticulously drawing from best practices and crafting valuable tools that you can use time and time again.

I started this book by sharing how much I was moved by the performance of Alma Deutscher. She taught me that I needed to give myself the permission and freedom to share my gifts and talents with the world...to shine bright. Without even knowing it, she curated a world-class learning experience, just for me. She gave me one of the greatest gifts of all because it can never be taken away from me. Unbeknownst to her, Alma taught me something that changed my life's course for the better.

May we all act with steadfast generosity when giving this beautiful gift to others.

Acknowledgements

Family and Friends

Thank you for being my number one fans and champions, encouraging me to shine bright, and always greeting me with grace and generosity. Thank you for believing in my talents and loving me without limits.

Bahaar Tadjbakhsh	James Terrell Campbell	Massy Sharifi
Rahmon Tadjbakhsh	Shahla Tadjbakhsh	Ray Tadjbakhsh
Ali Tadjbakhsh	Naseem Abolfathi	Andrea Caguioa
Niloofar Shaafi	Vannie Ly	Maggie Montgomery
Marisa Camisasca	Jessica Gerson	Rawand Ataya
Justin Patton	Roya Aghavali	Amrita Mukherji
Jennifer Szerlip	Alex Friedman	Rosanna Caguioa
Liz Marie	Sandra Ponce	Noah Baron Katchoeian
Jacquelyn Evancoe	Megan Ochoa	Kathy Suarez
Amir Katchoeian	Nader Katchoeian	Amal Nasri

References

Anderson, L.W., Krathwohl, D.R., Airasian, P.W., Cruikshank, K.A., Mayer, R.E., Pintrich, P.R., Raths, J., & Wittrock, M.C. (2001). *A Taxonomy for Learning, Teaching, and Assessing: A revision of Bloom's Taxonomy of Educational Objectives*.

Bloom, B.S., Engelhart, M.D., Furst, E.J., Hill, W.H., & Krathwohl, D.R. (1956). *Taxonomy of Educational Objectives: The Classification of Educational Goals*.

Knowles, M. (1990). *The Adult Learner* (4th Ed.).

Locke, E. A., & Latham, G. P. (1990). *A Theory of Goal Setting and Task Performance*.

Noe, R. A. (2017). *Employee Training and Development* (7th Ed.).

Learning and Development in Practice

TOOLKIT

Tadjbakhsh's 7-Step Process for High-Impact Training:

1. Client Intake

2. Learner Inquiry

3. Analysis and Insights

4. Learning Objective and Success Metrics

5. Session Blueprint

6. Program Deliverables

7. Training Launch and Follow-Up

Client Intake Meeting Checklist

Before the meeting

1. Email the client at least 48 hours prior to the meeting to confirm the date and time of your meeting. Confirm meeting address (in-person) or phone number/link (virtual) in your email.

    a. *See Client Intake Confirmation Template.*

2. Prepare an agenda and questions for the client intake meeting.

    a. *See Client Intake Meeting Guide.*

    b. *See Client Intake Meeting Question Bank.*

3. Prepare a training project roadmap with your standard/preferred timeline as a baseline.

    a. *See Example Training Roadmap.*

4. Ensure that you have all documents and note-taking materials handy.

5. Take a deep breath, smile, be pleasant, and get excited! You are going to help make your client's life better by adding value right away!

During the meeting

1. Utilize your agenda and questions to stay on track.

2. Understand the purpose and desired outcomes of the training from the client's perspective.

3. Manage expectations on the training project timeline and deliverables.

4. Establish clear next steps and ownership of action items.

5. Make an attempt to schedule 3-5 learner interviews.

After the meeting

1. Email the client within the next 24 hours (*see Client Intake Follow-Up Email Template*):

   a. Summarize the main points and training roadmap with due dates for key deliverables.

   b. Provide an outline of next steps.

   c. Confirm dates, times, and locations of upcoming learner interviews.

2. Follow up with the client as needed.

Client Intake Confirmation Template

In-Person Meeting – Email Confirmation Template:

Hi [Client's Name],

I hope all is well! I am looking forward to our meeting this [day of week], [date], [time] at [location/address].

Please do not hesitate to contact me if you need anything. Thank you and I hope you have a wonderful day!

See you soon,
[your name]
[best number to get in contact with you]

Phone Meeting – Email Confirmation Template:

Hi [Client's Name],

I hope all is well! I am looking forward to our call this [day of week], [date] at [time]. I will call you at [client's phone number].

Please do not hesitate to contact me if you need anything. Thank you and I hope you have a wonderful day!

Talk soon,
[your name]
[best number to get in contact with you]

Virtual Meeting – Email Confirmation Template:

Hi [Client's Name],

I hope all is well! I look forward to connecting with you this [day of week], [date], [time]. Details for joining the meeting can be found below.

[virtual meeting link/joining details]

Thank you and please do not hesitate to contact me if you need anything. I hope you have a wonderful day!

Talk soon,
[your name]

Example Training Roadmap

MON	TUE	WED	THUR	FRI
	Client Intake	Create Project Roadmap	Learner Inquiry	Learner Inquiry
Learner Inquiry	Learner Inquiry	Learner Inquiry	Analysis & Insights	Analysis & Insights
Analysis & Insights	Analysis & Insights	Analysis & Insights	Learning Objectives & Success Metrics	Learning Objectives & Success Metrics
Learning Objectives & Success Metrics	Learning Objectives & Success Metrics	Learning Objectives & Success Metrics	Learning Objectives & Success Metrics	Session Blueprint
Session Blueprint	Session Blueprint	Session Blueprint	Session Blueprint	Client Check-In
Program Deliverables	Program Deliverables	Program Deliverables	Program Deliverables	Program Deliverables
Program Deliverables	Client Check-In	Program Deliverables	Program Deliverables	Program Deliverables
	Training Launch			Client Follow-Up
Ongoing Follow-Ups as Needed				

Client Intake Meeting Guide

Meeting Agenda Template

Topic	Objective	Time
Welcome & Introduction	• Ask client how they're doing and "what's new" in their world to build rapport. • Introduce yourself and briefly summarize your credentials to build credibility. • State the purpose of the call. Review the agenda you prepared and what you hope to accomplish in the meeting. Ask client if it sounds like a good plan and if they have any questions.	3-5 minutes
Discovery	• Understand the purpose and desired outcomes of the training from the client's perspective. Try to uncover the problem they need help solving. • Ask the questions you prepared for the meeting (use Question Bank to prepare). Have an open dialogue.	30-35 minutes
	• Establish how you and the client will work together. • Manage expectations with the training project timeline by reviewing the Training Roadmap. • Achieve consensus on deadlines for key deliverables and activities. • Ask the client if they have any questions.	7-10 minutes

| Closing & Next Steps | • Establish clear next steps and ownership of action items.
• Make an attempt to schedule 3-5 learner interviews.
• Inform the client that you will email them a summary of the meeting's main points, their customized training roadmap, an outline of key next steps, and confirmation of upcoming learner interviews.
• Ask the client if they have any additional questions or if there is anything else they would like to discuss. | 5-10 minutes |

Client Intake Meeting Question Bank

Note: Questions are <u>not</u> listed in a preferred sequential order. Select the questions that will help you optimize your time with your client during the intake meeting. Modify and/or write your own questions accordingly. Bolded questions are highly recommended.

- What is the problem you are hoping to solve with training?
- Why do you believe training is part of the solution to the problem? Could there be other potential solutions that you have not yet explored or thought of as options?
- How will you, your team, and/or your organization benefit from solving this problem?
- What are the gaps between your current and ideal situation? What are the roadblocks?
- **What do you want learners to walk away with (learn) by the end of the session?**
- **What do you want learners to <u>do</u> after the session both short-term and long-term as a result of the learning experience?**
- **What are the desired outcomes that would indicate to you that the training was successful?**
- Who is the audience (learners) that will participate in the training?
  a. Demographics, number of people, job titles, locations, languages, educational background, characteristics, pain points, etc.
- How would you describe the learning culture of the organization (or culture in general)?
- How will learners be supported to sustain behaviors they learn as a result of the training?
- When are you looking to launch/host the training session(s)?

- How do you envision for the training to be rolled out?

- Do you have a preference for the modality in which training is delivered, e.g. in-person, virtual, or something else?

- What else would you like to share that we have not yet had a chance to talk about?

Client Intake Follow-Up Email Template

Hi [Client's Name],

I enjoyed connecting with you today! I am excited for our partnership and helping you launch [training topic/name] on [launch date]. As promised, I have enclosed our training roadmap which outlines key milestones, deadlines, and deliverables.

Here are the main points we covered:

- [business case + problem to be solved with training]
- [training audience/learner population]
- [what learners should walk away with/learn by the end of the training]
- [desired short-term and long-term learner behaviors as a result of training]
- [desired outcomes that indicate training was successful]

The next step is for me to conduct a series of interviews with 3-5 people from the training audience so that I can analyze and extract insights that will maximize the impact of the training in a customized, meaningful way for your employees. We confirmed the following:

- [Interview 1 date, time, location, etc.]
- [Interview 2 date, time, location, etc.]
- [Interview 3 date, time, location, etc.]

Once I complete the learner interviews and my analysis, I will prepare a training strategy for us to review the week of [date]. Please do not hesitate to contact me at any time.

Thank you very much and I hope you have a wonderful day! Talk soon.

Regards,
[your name]
[best number to get in contact with you]

Learner Problem & Hypothesized Solutions Template

Learner Problem Template	Hypothesized Solution Template
I need a way to [learner's need] because [insight].	By [doing something/creating a type of experience], then [this outcome].

Worksheet: Preparing for Your Interviews

Use this worksheet to prepare questions for your learner interviews. You can transfer them into your Learner Interview Guide once you've crafted your questions.

Learner Problem Template	Hypothesized Solution Template
I need a way to [learner's need] because [insight].	By [doing something/creating a type of experience], then [this outcome].

Interview Questions

Write down at least 5 interview questions that will help you test your hypothesis and learn more about your learner's pain points.

Interview Questions
[Question 1]
[Question 2]
[Question 3]
[Question 4]
[Question 5]

Learner Interview Guide

Use this template to prepare for your learner interviews. Print or save multiple versions so that you can use one for each interview. Be sure to adapt as needed and/or if there are multiple interviewers/note-takers.

Opening

"Hello, [interviewee's name]! Thank you for taking the time to meet with me today. My name is [your name] and I am partnering with [client's name] on a training project. My goal for today is to learn about your experiences and perspective in relation to [topic] so that we can take action to [what you will do, e.g., "improve your experience..."]. I have prepared a list of questions that I would love to cover, but really, today is about having more of a conversation. I am going to jot down some notes while we talk so that I make sure to capture your valuable insights. Also, I want to make sure you know that what you share with me today is completely confidential. This means that only I will have access to these notes and will never share your name and responses, only general comments I have collected from all the people I interview. With that being said, what questions do you have before we begin?"

Question	Interview Notes
[Question 1]	• [Note] • [Note]
[Question 2]	• [Note] • [Note]
[Question 3]	• [Note] • [Note]
[Question 4]	• [Note] • [Note]
[Question 5]	• [Note] • [Note]

Closing

"Great! Well, that brings us to the end of our discussion. I really appreciate you taking the time to meet with me today, [interviewee name]! In terms of next step, what you can expect is [next steps that are relevant to the learner]. Thank you again so much!"

Learning Objectives Worksheet

Learner Problem	Hypothesized Solution	Learning Objective

Success Metrics Worksheet

Learner Problem	Hypothesized Solution	Learning Objective
Success Metrics		

Session Blueprint Template

Topic	What to Cover	Learning Objective	Delivery Method	Materials	Facilitator	Time

Client Check-In Deck Outline

Topic	What to Cover	Time
Title Slide	• Project title • Date of check-in	Less than 1 min
Project Purpose	• Business case • Client's current state vs. desired state • Client intake summary • Date of training launch	2 min
Training Project Roadmap	• Use image of Training Roadmap and a star/marker/color indicating: "We are here!" on Client Check-In box	2 min
Learner Insights	• Number of interviews conducted • Emerging themes • Final learner problems and hypothesized solutions side-by-side	2 min
Learning Objectives & Success Metrics	• Use highlights from "Success Metrics Worksheet" to create this slide • Ask for client's thoughts on if metrics/key results are realistic and feasible	4 min
Session Blueprint	• Use highlights from "Session Blueprint" to create this slide • Do not show every single detail, just the highlights UNLESS the client asks to see it	2 min

Feedback + Q&A	• Ask for the client's reactions and questions • Gather feedback and answer questions	10 min
Next Steps	• Align on updates that will be made to training • Align on next steps • Confirm training session logistics as needed (e.g., who will print materials, is the training room booked, what else is needed, etc.) • Schedule final pre-launch check-in call with client approximately one week prior to training launch	5-7 min

Content Development Matrix Template

Literature Review					
Article Title/ Citation	Purpose of the Study/ Article	Key Findings/ Takeaways	Strengths	Limita-tions	Applica-tion to Training Session
[Article 1]					
[Article 2]					
[Article 3]					
[Article 4]					
[Article 5]					

5+ key principles you will include in your training	Learning Objective

Client Follow-Up Meeting Guide

Meeting Agenda Template

Topic	Objective	Time
Welcome	• Ask client how they're doing. • State the purpose of the call. Review the agenda you prepared and what you hope to accomplish in the meeting. Ask the client if it sounds like a good plan and if they have any questions.	2 min
Training Retrospective	• Ask for the client's reactions and what they have been hearing about the training session questions. • Ask for feedback: What went well, what could have been improved, and what were some areas of untapped potential to consider for future training iterations.	10-15 min
Success Metrics & Sustainment Planning	• Inquire about the client's plans for sustainment in order to promote training transfer. • Provide suggestions and weave in evaluating the success metrics so that the client can optimize the return on their investment. • Ask the client if they have any questions.	10-15 min
Client Satisfaction & Next Steps	• Ask the client what else there is that you can do to support them. Ask how they are feeling about the investment they made in the training.	7-10 min

- Ask the client if they have any additional questions or if there is anything else they would like to discuss.
- Establish next steps.

Made in the USA
Coppell, TX
31 May 2024

32946187R00073